MODERN HOHMANN-WOHLFAHRT
for Violin — Volume II

MODERN *Hohmann-Wohlfahrt* is a compilation of two of the world's most famous methods for violin, entirely revised, re-edited and re-styled to meet the demands of modern education. For more than fifty years the instructional works of both Hohmann and Wohlfahrt have enjoyed unequalled popularity with the foremost violin pedagogues of Europe and America.

THE *string by string* approach, utilized in the Hohmann method, is unquestionably the easiest means ever devised for teaching violin. Likewise, the approach followed by Hohmann in commencing on the E string, and proceeding in logical order from the E to the A string, from the A to the D string, and from the D to the G string, has proved itself, through years of practical application, to be the most satisfactory of all plans for teaching violin. Furthermore, Hohmann's extensive use of melodic material, particularly at a time when other writers of violin methods were making use chiefly of dry, technical studies in their own works, has established him, beyond all question, as one of the world's most important pioneers in the field of music pedagogy.

THE name *Wohlfahrt* is known to violinists everywhere. Symbolic of the best in easy studies for the violin, the name of this noted writer is respected far and wide, and the famous *Wohlfahrt Elementary Method for Violin* has enjoyed a reputation second only to that of the famous *Hohmann Violin Method.*

THE original editions of these justly celebrated works, abounding in a wealth of valuable material that has proved indispensable in violin study for over half a century, have been carefully consulted in preparing the present work. All of the technical and melodic material taken from Book I of Hohmann. as well as from the Wohlfahrt beginners' method, has been arranged in a graded, progressive sequence, and appears in Volume I of the present series. Volume II of *Modern Hohmann-Wohlfahrt* contains material selected from Books II and III of the original Hohmann edition, in addition to choice etudes selected from the various elementary books written by Wohlfahrt. Volume I of the present series covers the first position through the major keys of C, G, F, D and B♭, while Volume II reviews these keys, takes up the additional major keys of A and E♭, and introduces the player to the minor keys related to the major keys already studied. Volume II also takes up such technical necessities as sixteenth notes, the dotted eighth note followed by a sixteenth note, syncopation, staccato playing, double stops, and chords. Upon the completion of Volumes I and II of the *Modern Hohmann-Wohlfahrt* method, the player is ready to commence the study of the third position on the violin, and for this purpose, he should turn to the pages of *Introducing the Positions, Volume I,* which is, in reality, a continuation of the present course of study.

IN conclusion, the writer takes pleasure in dedicating the present work to *Mr. Will Hays,* eminent violinist and pedagogue, and former member of the *San Francisco Symphony Orchestra,* whose picture appears in the first volume of the *Modern Hohmann-Wohlfahrt.* It was this excellent teacher, who many years ago, used the *Hohmann Violin Method* to give the writer his first instruction on the instrument.

Harvey S. Whistler, Ph. D.

Key of C Major

Scale of C Major

Chord of C Major

1

Also practice (1) slurring each four tones, and (2) slurring each eight tones.

EXERCISE

HOHMANN

2

RHYTHMICAL STUDY

HOHMANN

3

TECHNIC BUILDER

HOHMANN

4

Menuet
(Duet)

SPOHR-HOHMANN

Andante

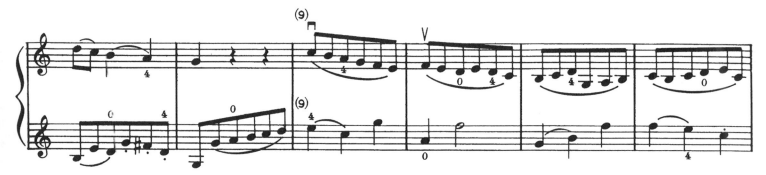

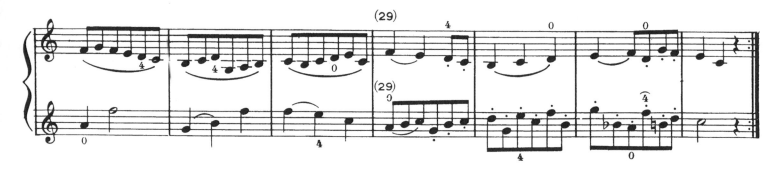

Legato and Staccato

LEGATO BOWINGS
(To be practiced in a smooth, connected manner)

STACCATO BOWINGS
(To be practiced in a short, detached manner)

Bowing Etude

WOHLFAHRT

Developing Double-Stops

Key of G Major

Scale of G Major (Practice both parts.)   Chord of G Major

14

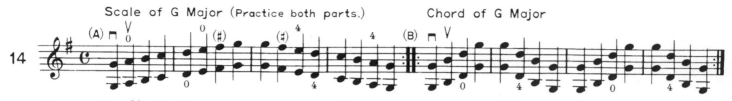

Also practice (1) slurring each four tones, and (2) slurring each eight tones.

EXERCISE

HOHMANN

15

GRACE - NOTES

HOHMANN

16

GRACE - NOTE STUDY

HOHMANN

17

Grace-Note Scherzo
(Duet)

WOHLFAHRT

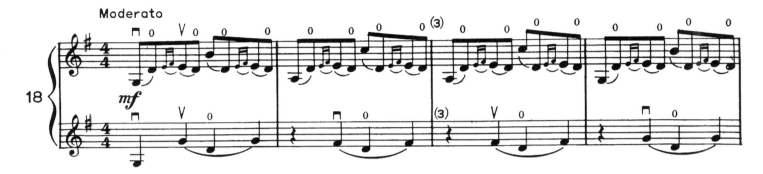

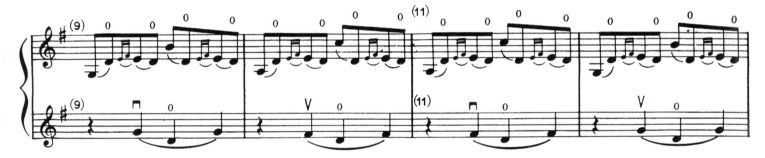

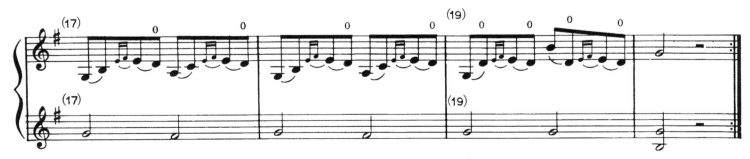

Sixteenth Notes

Sixteenth Note Etude

WOHLFAHRT

Also practice (1) using a separate bow for each tone, (2) slurring each two tones, (3) slurring each four tones, and (4) slurring each eight tones.

QUARTER AND SIXTEENTH NOTES ALTERNATED

WB = Whole Bow

Rhythmical Etude

WOHLFAHRT

Developing Chords

THREE NOTE CHORDS

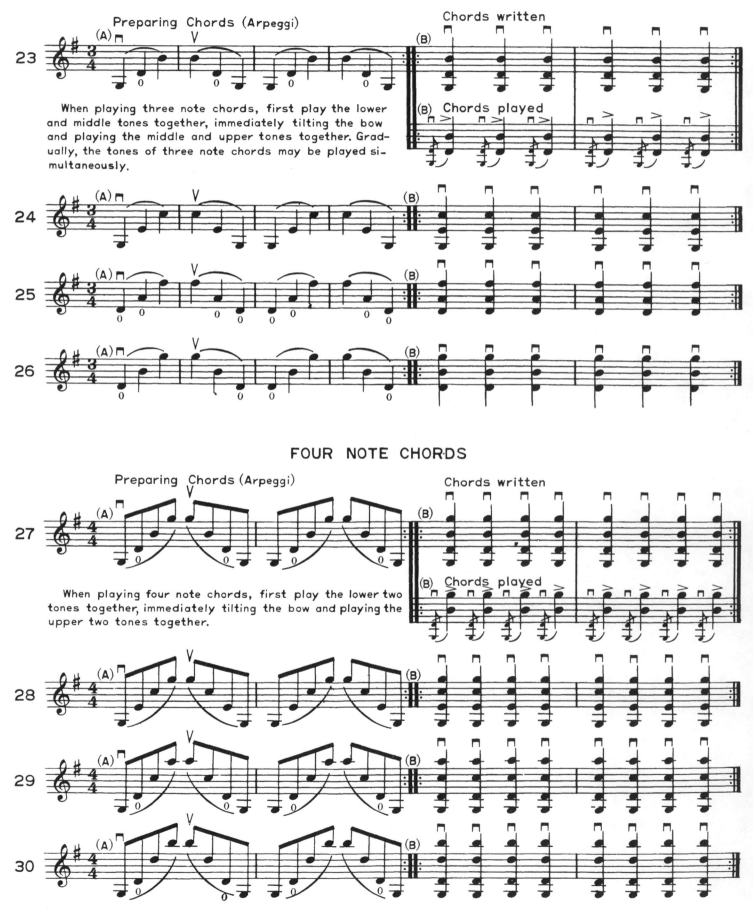

When playing three note chords, first play the lower and middle tones together, immediately tilting the bow and playing the middle and upper tones together. Gradually, the tones of three note chords may be played simultaneously.

FOUR NOTE CHORDS

When playing four note chords, first play the lower two tones together, immediately tilting the bow and playing the upper two tones together.

Pizzicato

PIZZICATO, or PIZZ. = Pluck the string with the first finger.

ARCO, or CON ARCO = Produce the tone with the bow.

In producing the tone by plucking the string (PIZZICATO), use the first finger of the right hand, placing the thumb of that hand against the end of the fingerboard, in order to lend support to the movement.

Pizzicato Duet

GRÜN

Key of F Major

Scale of F Major   Chord of F Major

32

Also practice (1) slurring each four tones, and (2) slurring each eight tones.

EXERCISE

HOHMANN

33

GRACE - NOTE STUDY

WOHLFAHRT

34

Melodic Etude

WOHLFAHRT

Also practice (1) pizzicato, and (2) slurring each complete measure in one bow.

Syncopation Patterns

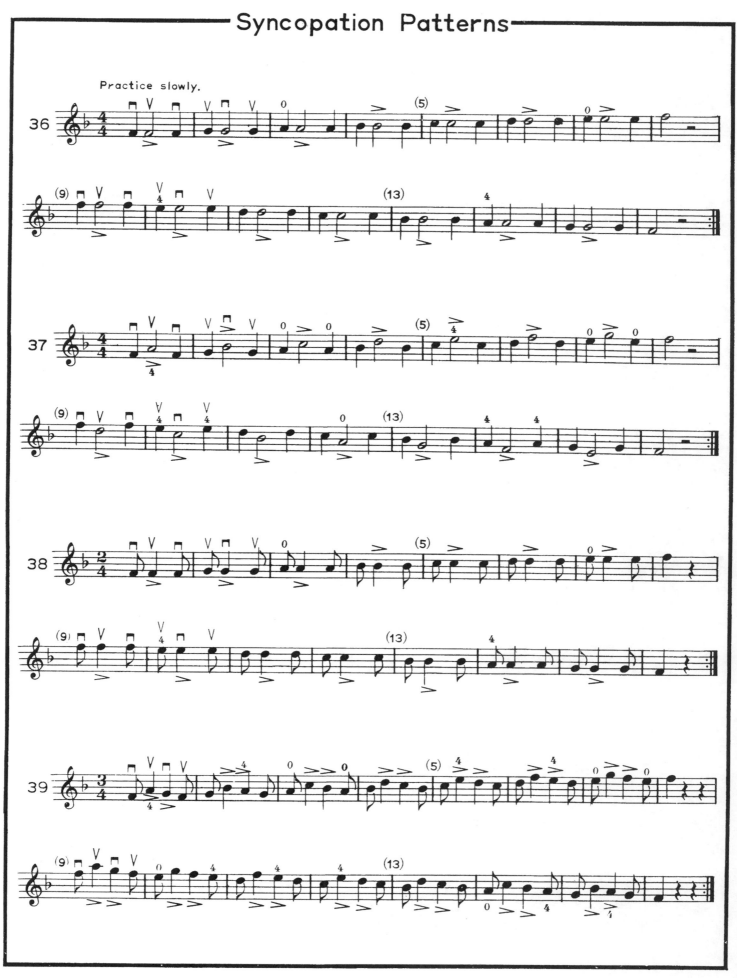

Syncopated Etude No.1

WOHLFAHRT

Before playing as written, practice with all separate bows.

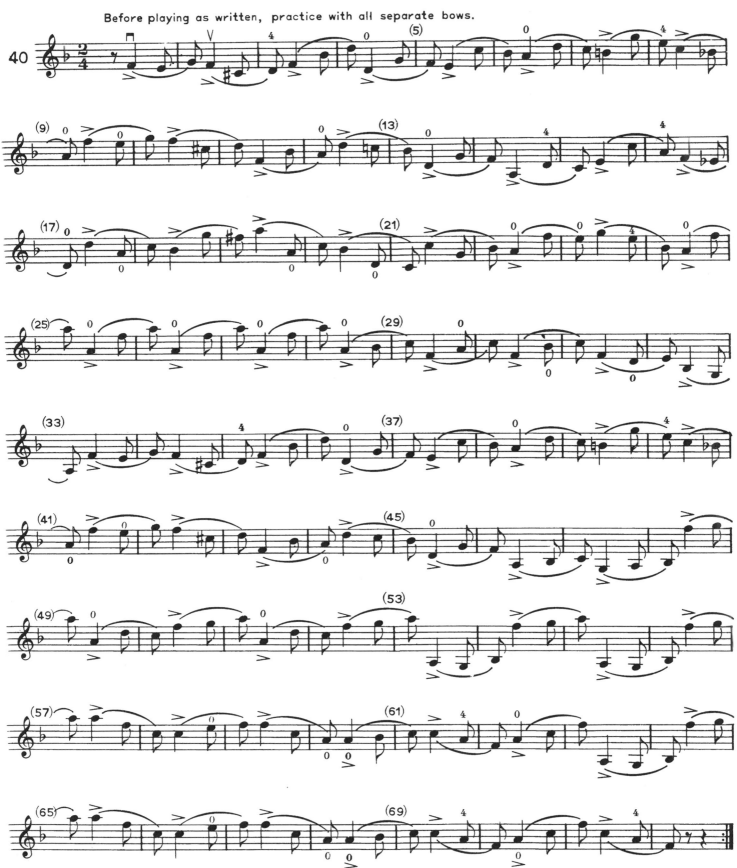

Key of D Major

41

Scale of D Major   Chord of D Major

Also practice (1) slurring each four tones, and (2) slurring each eight tones.

EXERCISE

HOHMANN

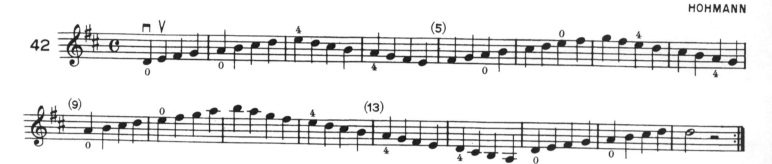

42

TECHNIC BUILDER

HOHMANN

43

BASIC STUDY

HOHMANN

44

THE DOTTED EIGHTH NOTE FOLLOWED BY A SIXTEENTH NOTE

45

Count 1 & a 2 & a 3 & a 4 & a   1   2   3   4

Dotted Eighth Note Etude No. 1

WOHLFAHRT

46

Syncopated Melody
(Duet)

ALARD

Staccato Etude No. 1

WOHLFAHRT

Before practicing this etude, review staccato bowings on Bowing Etude, No.6, page 4.

Staccato Etude No. 2

Before practicing this etude, review staccato bowings on Bowing Etude, No. 6, page 4.

WOHLFAHRT

Key of B♭ Major

Scale of B♭ Major (Practice both parts.)   Chord of B♭ Major

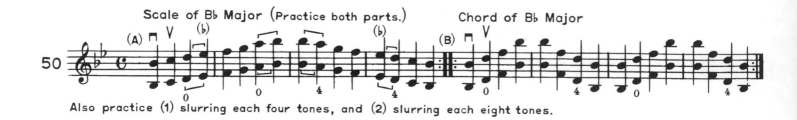

50

Also practice (1) slurring each four tones, and (2) slurring each eight tones.

EXERCISE

HOHMANN

51

FINGER CROSSING STUDY

DANCLA

Do not raise the 1st finger; cross the 2nd finger over the 1st.

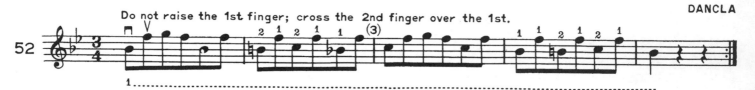

52

STRING CROSSING STUDY
(Octaves)

HOHMANN

53

TECHNIC BUILDER

WOHLFAHRT

54

22

Triplet Etude

BÖHMER

Also practice pizzicato.

Dotted Eighth Note Etude No. 2

BÖHMER

March from Aida
(Duet)

VERDI

Maestoso

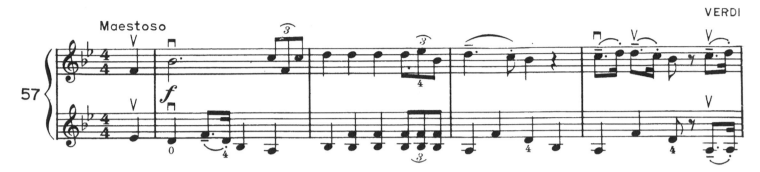

Key of A Major

Scale of A Major (Practice both parts.)   Chord of A Major

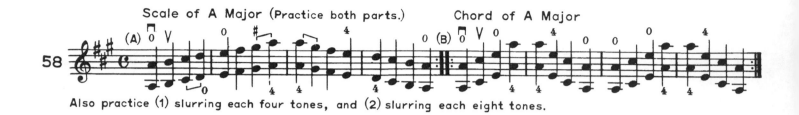

58

Also practice (1) slurring each four tones, and (2) slurring each eight tones.

EXERCISE

HOHMANN

59

FOUNDATION STUDY

HOHMANN

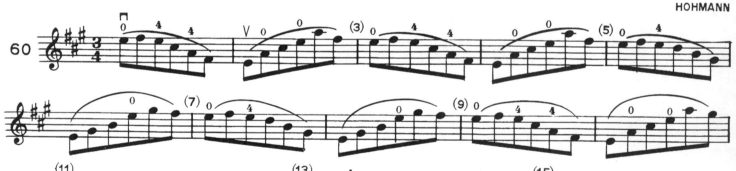

60

TECHNIC BUILDER

HOHMANN

61

Legato Etude

BÖHMER

Also practice (1) with a separate bow for each tone, (2) slurring each four tones, (3) slurring each complete measure, and (4) pizzicato.

Pastorale
(Duet)

WICHTL

Canzonetta
(Duet)

MAZAS

Allegro de Concert
(Duet)

Also practice with a separate bow for each tone.

SPOHR - HOHMANN

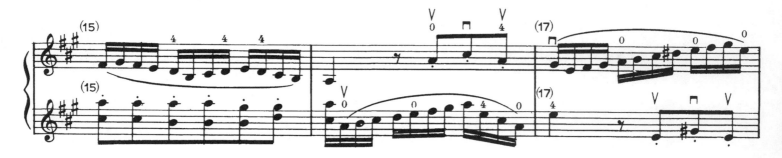

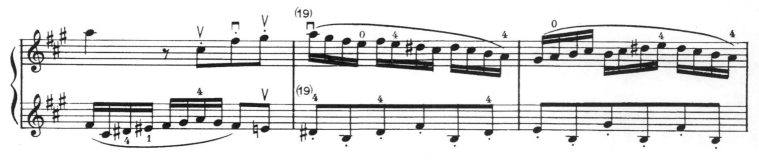

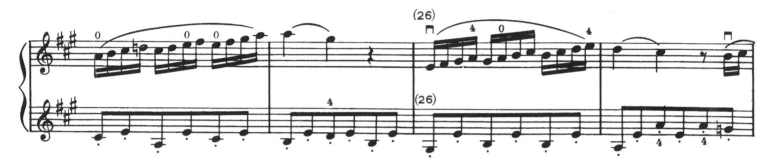

Key of E♭ Major

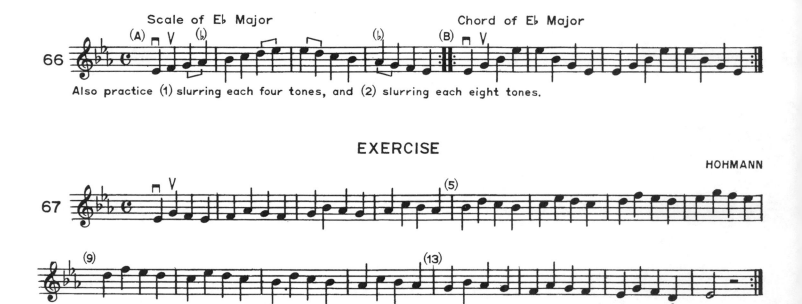

66 Scale of E♭ Major · Chord of E♭ Major

Also practice (1) slurring each four tones, and (2) slurring each eight tones.

EXERCISE

HOHMANN

67

TRIPLET STUDY

HOHMANN

68

CHORDS

WOHLFAHRT

69

70

71

Tremolo Etude

WOHLFAHRT

Play as many down and up bows as possible on each note. Use upper part of bow.

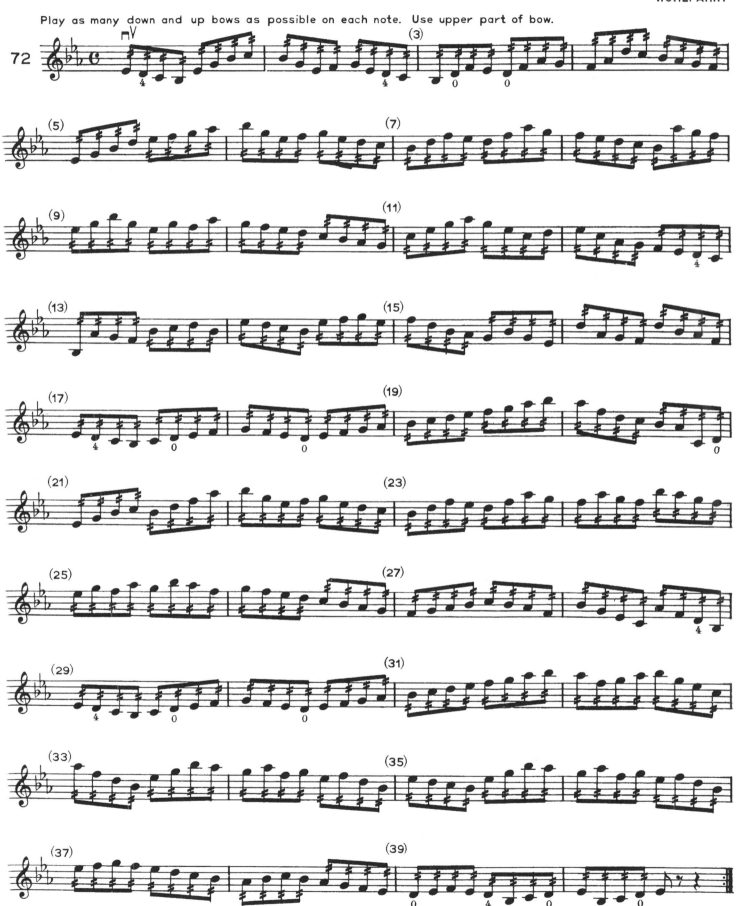

Etude de Concertante

SCHUBERT

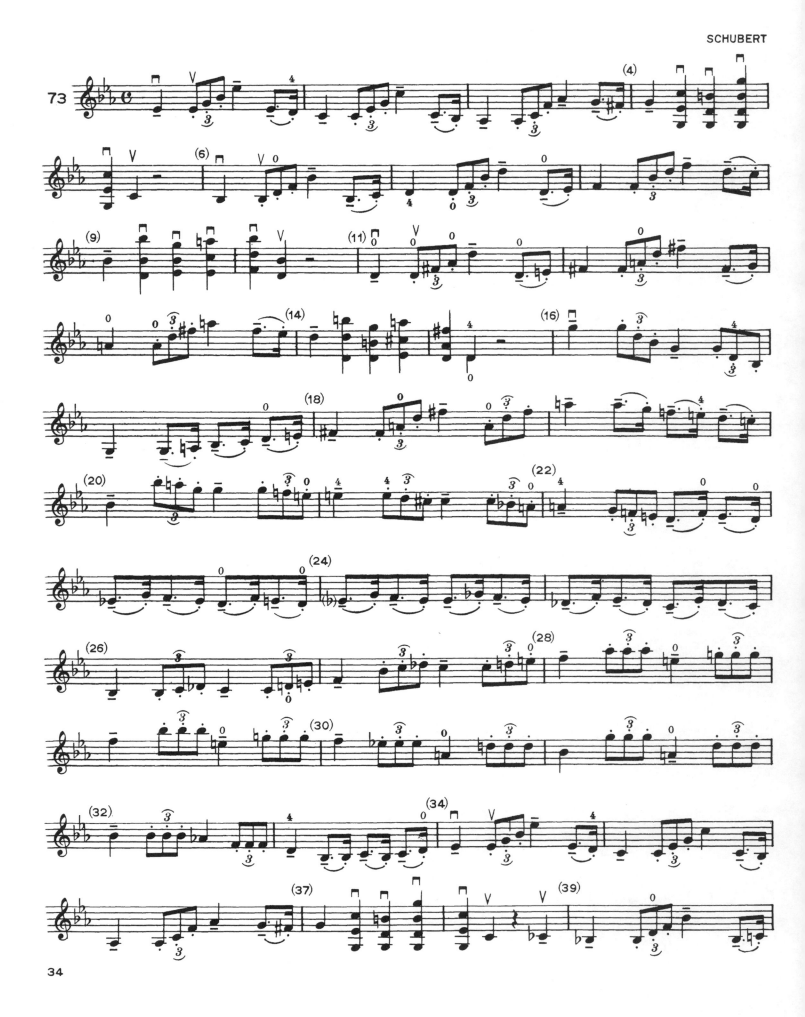

Chromatics

CHROMATIC SCALE

HOHMANN

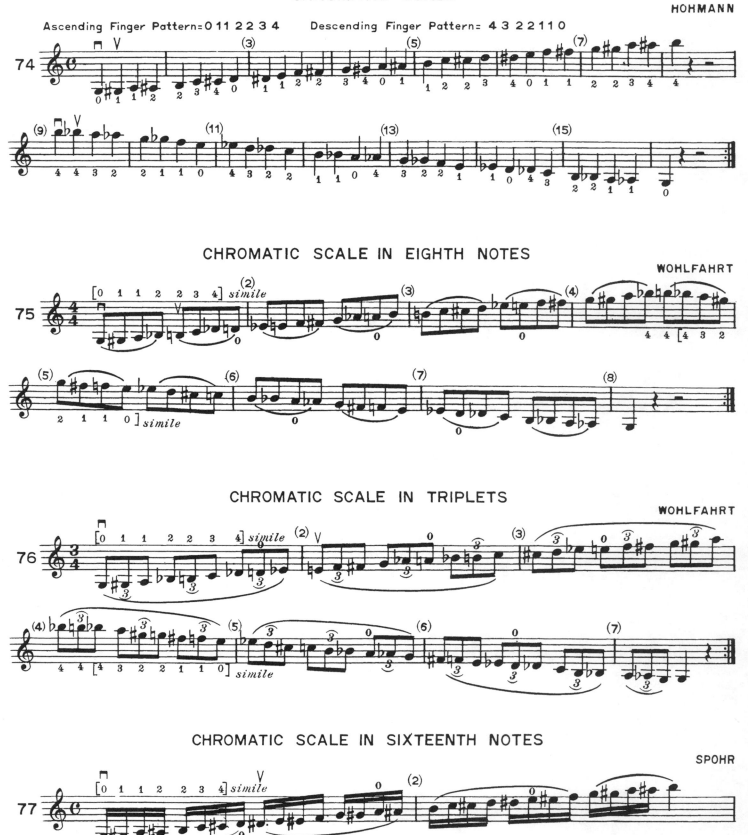

CHROMATIC SCALE IN EIGHTH NOTES

WOHLFAHRT

CHROMATIC SCALE IN TRIPLETS

WOHLFAHRT

CHROMATIC SCALE IN SIXTEENTH NOTES

SPOHR

Key of A Minor

(Relative to the Key of C Major)

Scale of A Harmonic Minor (Practice both parts)   Scale of A Melodic Minor

78

Also practice (1) slurring each four tones, and (2) slurring each eight tones.

EXERCISE

HOHMANN

79

ADVANCED EXERCISE

HOHMANN

80

Key of E Minor
(Relative to the Key of G Major)

Scale of E Harmonic Minor   Scale of E Melodic Minor

81

Also practice (1) slurring each four tones, and (2) slurring each eight tones.

Minor Key Etude No. 1

WOHLFAHRT

82

Key of D Minor
(Relative to the Key of F Major)

Scale of D Harmonic Minor   Scale of D Melodic Minor

83

Also practice (1) slurring each four tones, and (2) slurring each eight tones.

EXERCISE

HOHMANN

84

frog

Minor Key Etude No. 2

Also practice (1) slurring each four tones, (2) slurring each eight tones, and (3) pizzicato.

BÖHMER

85

Key of B Minor
(Relative to the Key of D Major)

Scale of B Harmonic Minor (Practice both parts.) Scale of B Melodic Minor

Also practice (1) slurring each four tones, and (2) slurring each eight tones.

Caprice

HOHMANN

Key of G Minor

(Relative to the Key of B♭ Major)

Scale of G Harmonic Minor (Practice both parts) Scale of G Melodic Minor

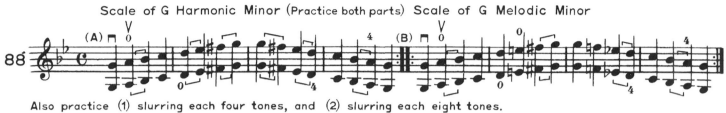

Also practice (1) slurring each four tones, and (2) slurring each eight tones.

Syncopated Etude No. 2

WOHLFAHRT

Before practicing this etude, review (1) syncopation pattern in exercise No. 38, page 14, and (2) Syncopated Etude, No. 40, page 15.

Key of F♯ Minor
(Relative to the Key of A Major)

Scale of F♯ Harmonic Minor   Scale of F♯ Melodic Minor

90

Also practice (1) slurring each four tones, and (2) slurring each eight tones.

EXERCISE

HOHMANN

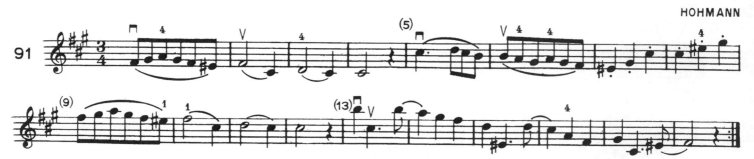

91

Chanson Triste
(Duet)

WICHTL

92

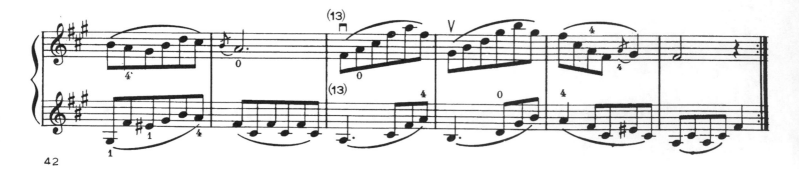

Key of C Minor
(Relative to the Key of E♭ Major)

Scale of C Harmonic Minor   Scale of C Melodic Minor

93

Also practice (1) slurring each four tones, and (2) slurring each eight tones.

EXERCISE

HOHMANN

94

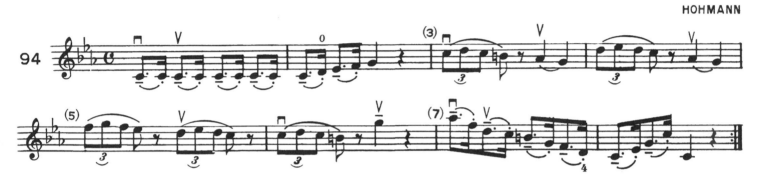

Dramatic Episode
(Duet)

WICHTL

95

Double-Stops and Chords

SIXTHS

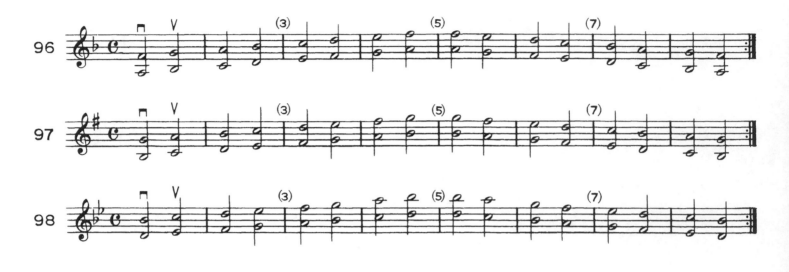

OCTAVES

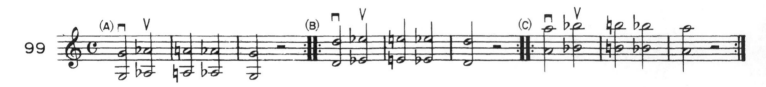

SIXTHS AND OCTAVES

THIRDS

EXERCISES IN THIRDS

THIRDS, FOURTHS AND SIXTHS

SINGLE-STOPS AND OPEN STRINGS

CHORDS

Chorale
(Duet)

GRÜN

45

Double-Stop Etude

ALARD

Double-Stop and Chord Etude

WOHLFAHRT

Processional
(Duet)

TOURS

Extending the Fourth Finger

4̂= Fourth finger extended. Do not move the hand forward. Instead, merely stretch the fourth finger until it is forward sufficiently to reach the desired tone. Keep the 1st, 2nd and 3rd fingers down while extending the 4th finger.

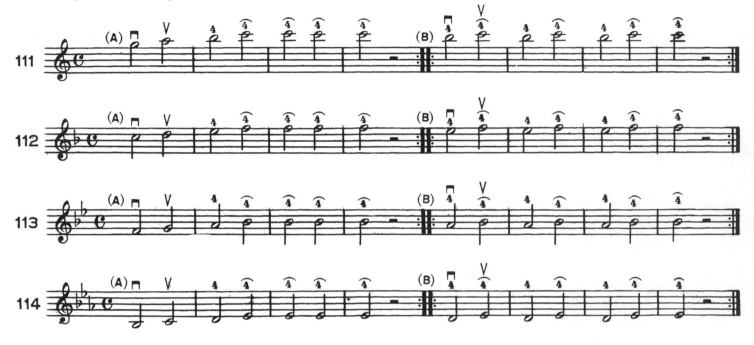

SCALE WITH FOURTH FINGER EXTENSION

FINGER EXTENSION EXERCISES

Finger Extension Etude

WOHLFAHRT

Wohlfahrt Daily Finger Exercises

Raise fingers high and strike them forcefully on the string. Practice slowly at first; later increase the tempo of each exercise. Keep all fingers down as long as possible.

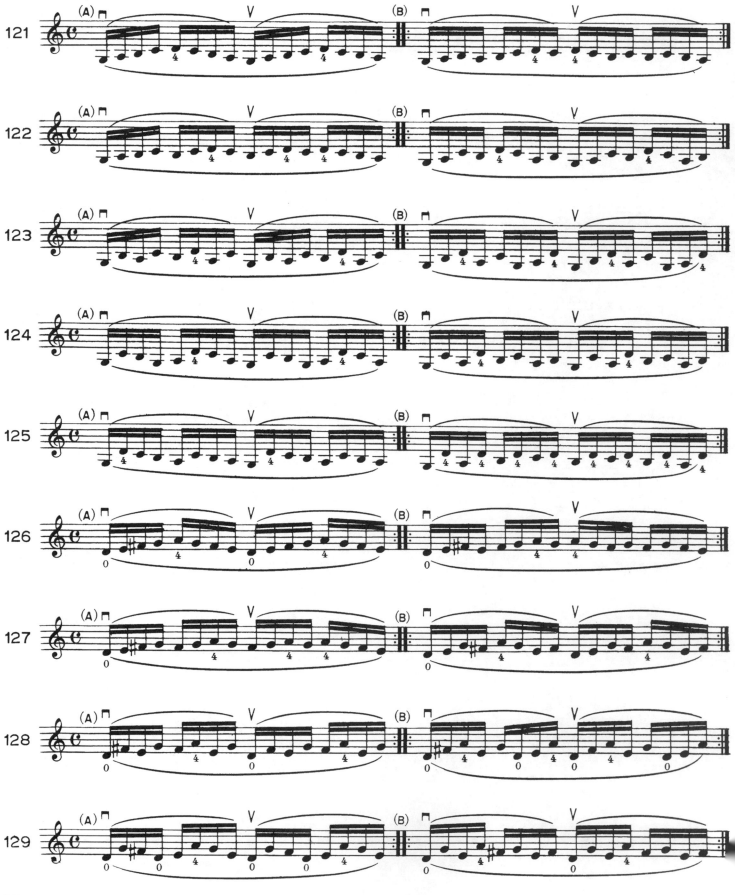

Preparatory Trill Exercises

Raise fingers high and strike the forcefully on the string. Practice slowly at first; later, increase the tempo of each exercise. Keep all fingers down as long as possible.

Stretching and Strengthening the Fourth Finger

Keep the 1st, 2nd, and 3rd fingers down while stretching the 4th finger.

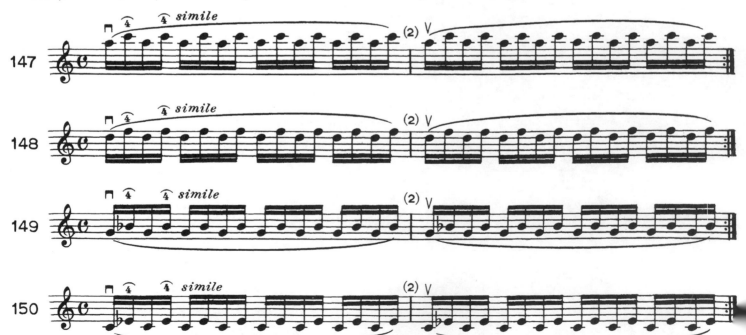

The Trill

WHOLE NOTE EXAMPLE

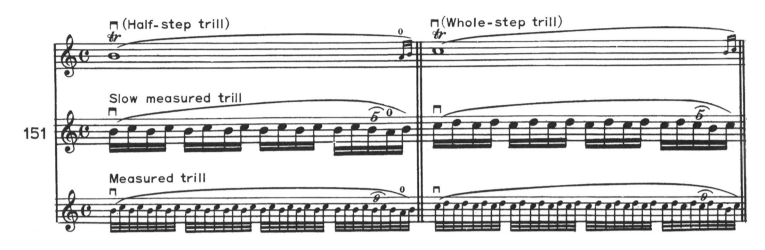

HALF NOTE EXAMPLE

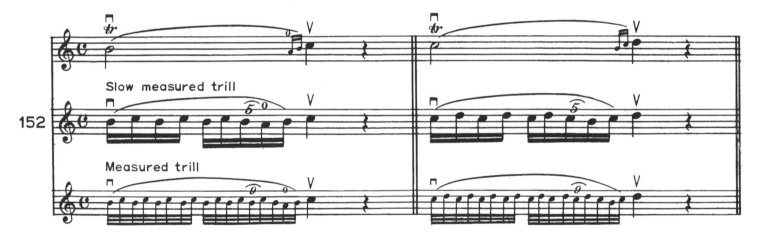

Trill Exercises

It does not matter how many notes each of the following trills contains; the greater the number of notes in a trill, the better the trill will sound.

Trill Etude

WOHLFAHRT

Trill Duet

TOURS

Coronation March
(Processional)

WOHLFAHRT

The Fountain
(Arpeggio Duet)

In playing arpeggi, use open strings wherever possible.

SCHUBERT

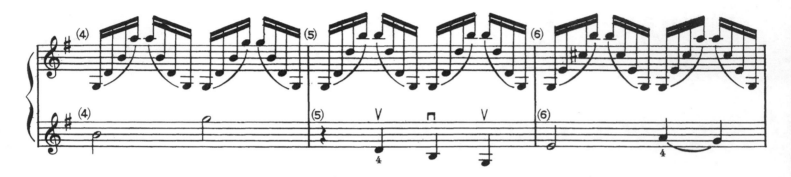

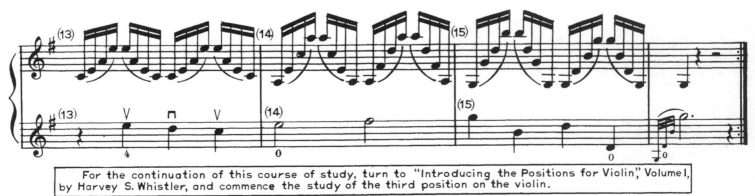

For the continuation of this course of study, turn to "Introducing the Positions for Violin," Volume I, by Harvey S. Whistler, and commence the study of the third position on the violin.